THE TOTALED HANDYMAN

THE TOTALED HANDYMAN

By STAN KANN

Illustrated by Bill Davis

Published by J. P. Tarcher, Inc., Los Angeles
Distributed by St. Martin's Press, New York

To **Phyllis Diller** who started the whole
thing and who was the first one to discover
that I was out of this world and would have
trouble finding my way back

Copyright © **1980 by Stan Kann**
All rights reserved.
Library of Congress Catalog Card No.: 79-66309
Distributor's ISBN: 0-312-90894-6
Publisher's ISBN: 0-87477-115-3

Illustration: **Bill Davis**
Design: **John Bregna**

Manufactured in the United States of America

Published by J.P. Tarcher, Inc.
9110 Sunset Blvd., Los Angeles, Calif. 90069

Published simultaneously in Canada by Thomas Nelson & Sons Limited,
81 Curlew Drive, Don Mills, Ontario M3A 2R1

10 9 8 7 6 5 4 3 2 1
First Edition

Contents

OLD TILE

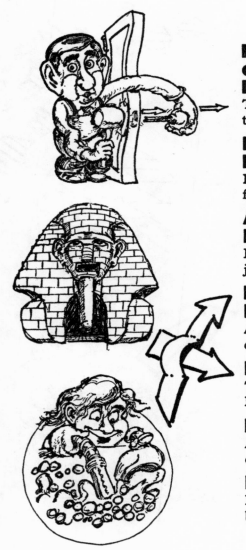

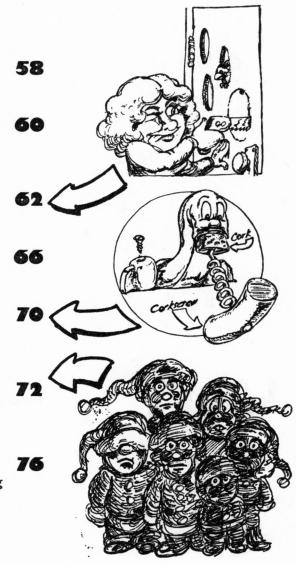

To Eyebolt
To Eyebolt
To Eyebolt

Outline Pool shape with string

Introduction

Hello and congratulations. You now have in your possession the handiest book you will ever own dealing with simple ways to repair things around your house.

I must make it clear at this point that I do not give advice on domestic problems, just do-it-yourself projects, so I would appreciate it if you wouldn't bother me about your impossible spouse, your runaway kid, crazy uncle, or foul-mouthed mother-in-law. During my short marriage, I found out that relative problems were absolute and couldn't be handled in a book of this kind. If the demand is great enough, I will consider putting out a book on domestic relations, but until then, keep your hard-luck stories to yourself.

I would like to thank a few people for their help and ideas, which have made this extraordinary book possible. I would like to but I can't, because I don't know who they are. For example, I never did get the name of the fellow who missed the turn at the corner and ran his car headlong into the side of my house, raising one end off the foundation. But I sure did learn a lot from the experience (see chapter on "How to Fix Sagging Walls and Floors").

And what can I tell you about the neighbor who raised all kinds of hell when he found out I had built my new garage on his property instead of my own? While I was on vacation, he had two cranes come out and put my new garage on top of my one-story house. This never would have occurred to me as a solution to the problem. I was very angry at first, of course, but then I got the idea for the chapter "Adding a Second Floor to a One-Story Flat Roof House."

During the months that followed, I tried to figure out how to get my car off the roof and saved many dollars in gas and much wear and tear on my Nash. Of course, the car was almost a total loss when the bad wind storm came along and blew the whole thing off the roof and into a neighbor's yard. But later on, I found out about Krazy Glue and how it would have prevented wind damage. The manufacturer claims that one drop will hold up to a ton but I think that 5,000 lbs. is closer to it. The significance of this information will become apparent as you read on. Live and learn.

And it was Halloween night when I discovered the secret about chimney cleaning. Some nasty children in my neighborhood thought they could frighten me by dropping in unannounced through my chimney. When they did, a wonderful new chimney-sweeping system was born. After they got out of the hospital and the word got around, I couldn't get any neighborhood kids to do it again until I came up with the Santa Claus helper story (see chapter on "Desooting and Cleaning House Chimney"). Since the pranksters were too soot-covered for identification, I never did find out who they were, but I'm grateful anyway.

And thanks also to Alvera, my devoted cleaning lady, who was taken from us only too soon. It was Alvera—not me—who created the whirlpool in a bathtub using a vacuum cleaner. One day while she was trying to clean the drapes on the bathroom window, she accidentally dropped the vacuum into the tub full of soaking clothes. That wasn't too bad, but she made the mistake of reaching into the water to get it. After the funeral, I realized that had it been only the hose instead of the whole cleaner in the water there would have been no funeral, since the hose, which is rubber or plastic, does not carry electricity. So when you are enjoying your vacuum whirlpool bath, think of that devoted cleaning lady who did not completely understand Edison's theory of electricity.

I have been asked to do another book just on household hints, and I will, just as soon as I locate my publisher. I went to his office with the new material, but his office is boarded up tight with no forwarding address.

Goodbye and thank you.

Stan Kann

Installing a
Sunken Tub in a Bathroom

Tools and Supplies Bathtub, chisel, saw, eyehooks, picture hanging wire, Krazy Glue, masonry drill, 4 insured people with heavy gloves.

The Romans knew how to live. They always had a sunken tub to bathe in, and so can you, with a lot less effort than you might suppose. You can do it yourself in an afternoon that will provide many amusing anecdotes for you and your friends. *But don't ask the landlord.*

First, you must get the tub loose from where it is standing. If you live in a poorly kept apartment building it may already be loose, in

which case you're way ahead of the game. If not, with a chisel, scrape out all the grout around the edge of the tub until the tub is as loose as it would be if you were lucky enough to live in a poorly kept apartment. Most tubs have the water taps in the wall, so you don't have to worry about the pipes now, except for the drain, and gravity will soon take care of that.

When the tub is loose, drill a hole in each corner with a masonry drill. Then take out your dusty surveying tools and put an eye-hook *directly* above each hole in the ceiling, applying one drop of Krazy Glue on each hook before you screw it into place.

You will need about 48 ft. of picture wire, 12 for each corner. Wrap one end through each hole and secure it. Run the other end through the hook in the ceiling. Have your 4 insured friends with gloves hold one of the wires and chat amiably while you cut a hole in the floor around the tub. Just before you finish, tell them, "I'm

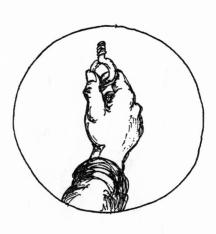

13

Run wire through holes at least 2 times

Wrap wire tightly around itself

almost through," because after the hole is made in the floor, the tub will have a tendency to fall into the apartment below. (Gravity, you know—unless you live in an area without gravity.) *The people holding the wires are supposed to prevent that.* No matter what happens, each person should somehow hold on to his wire until the tub top is flush with the floor and then wrap the picture wire tightly around itself and tie it off with a standard tub-securing knot. If you and your friends did it right, the tub will be *very securely in place;* if you didn't, that's your tough luck!

Okay, you now have a sunken tub, but so do your neighbors downstairs, only theirs is on their ceiling. You may want to explain to them that they mustn't worry about the bottom of your tub in

their apartment. Tell them you'll have a decorator come out and show them how to fix it so that no one will notice. You might invite them up for a bath.

Warning Do not fill tub with more than 20,000 lbs. of water and/or people, as the four drops of Krazy Glue will only hold that amount.

Oh, yes, the drain and other pipes. Call in a plumber. At all costs, you should avoid undertaking home repairs that might be better done by a professional.

OLD TILE

Replacing Damaged Floor Tiles

Tools and Supplies New floor tiles, electric iron, Krazy Glue, blowtorch, knife, freshly laundered clothes, asbestos gloves and knee pads.

Sometimes a section of tile comes loose on the floor or gets damaged in some way and must be replaced. First, the old tile must be loosened enough to be pried up from the floor, and heating is the very best way to do this.

Light the blowtorch as directed. Hold the torch close to the bad tile until it gets soft and loose (the tile, not the torch). Depending on how soft it gets, pry it up with a knife, spoon, or sponge.

Too Soft!

Warning Blowtorch must be pointed away from your body at all times to do the most good. If you don't think you can remember that, don't try this repair but place scatter rugs over damaged tile and go watch the "Gong Show." If tile catches on fire, you held torch far too close, so go watch the "Gong Show," too.

If you don't have a blowtorch, heat the tile with an electric iron. I recommend putting on the floor some clothes that you were going to iron anyway. This is a perfect chance to iron the clothes and get the tile loose at the same time. Don't spend too much time ironing. One shirt should do it.

Glue → Back of Tile

After you have the old tile out, fit the new tile into place. If it is a bit too large, you can trim it with a knife or sandpaper. Don't trim too much or you will have to throw it away and start a new one. After the new tile fits into the opening, put a drop of Krazy Glue on the back and press it into the hole. Then stand on the tile for a few moments until it sets.

Warning Be very, very careful not to get any Krazy Glue on the bottom of your shoes or the top of the new tile, because when you stand on it you won't be able to get loose. Krazy Glue holds up to 5,000 shouts and curses.

Now that you are finished yelling, unlace your shoe and step out. For a unique conversation piece in the center of the floor, you can make a planter out of it. For additional safety at night, it should be covered with luminous paint so you don't fall over your own foot.

Fixing Sticking Drawers

Tools and Supplies Eyehooks, wall, Krazy Glue, string, closet door, dresser with stuck drawer.

Have you ever stood there looking at your jammed drawers and wondering, "Why me?" If it's stuck shut because you put in one too many cantaloupes, there is nothing to be ashamed of. If it's too many pancakes—shame on you! Without being too judgmental, here's a quick way to get the drawer open (or closed) without calling a cabinetmaker.

Screw an eyehook into the drawer so it is right in the middle. Next, locate a wall directly across from the dresser drawer. If you can't find it, ask someone who is a better looker than you are.

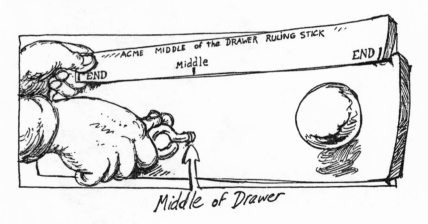

Middle of Drawer

When he finds it, screw another eyehook into the wall, making sure it's good and tight. Put one drop of Krazy Glue on the hook to make certain it holds tightly in the wall. Your drawer should not weigh more than 5,000 lbs.

Now, take a heavy piece of string and tie it through the eyehook in the dresser drawer. Run the string across the room and through the eyehook on the opposite wall. Find a door on the same side of the room the dresser is on, such as a closet door or the door to the room itself. If the door is on the opposite side of the room from the

Instant Replay
of OVERHAND WINDSOR
KNOT

dresser, then you will not need the eyehook in the wall across from the dresser but go right from the drawer to the door handle. Do Not Pass Go and Do Not Collect $200. Got that?

After you run the string through the hook across from the dresser, pull it tight and back across the room to the door handle. With the door in the open position, tie the string securely around the door handle, using an overhand Windsor knot. Then, with all your might, slam the door. It will pull the string and that will pull the

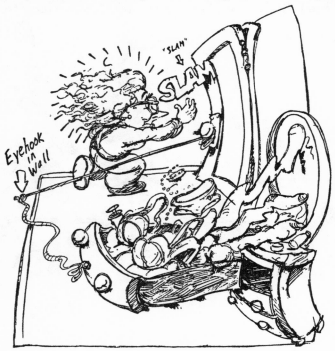

drawer across the room from the hook in the wall. Even if you don't *understand* the mechanics of this, just slam the door and *watch* the drawer fly open.

If the drawer is stuck open instead of closed, just turn the dresser to face the wall with the drawer touching the wall. Get a running start and slam yourself up against the back of the dresser. The drawer *will* close.

Warning This procedure can be dangerous if you are over sixty-five or wear a pacemaker. In either case, leave the drawer open and try to be philosophical about it.

For Drawer Stuck in Open Position...

Get a Running Start...

Dresser

WALL

Face dresser & open drawer towards wall

Installing a Pet Entrance in a Door

Tools and Supplies Dog, cat, saw, swing hinges, Krazy Glue.

Dogs are just like people in that they can't walk through walls. They also need a sense of personal freedom, which can only be obtained by either giving them a key to the house or apartment or building a special door. As it's unlikely they would know what to do with a key, build the door.

Door for Small Dog For a small dog you will want the door near the bottom so he or she can push it open and go in and out at will. Measure the dog in width and height (length not important). If dog jumps around while you are trying to get measurement, use the command "Stay" or give him a tranquilizer.

With a saw cut out a section near the bottom of the door that will look like a small-size-animal door. Take the hinge and put one drop of Krazy Glue on both sides of it. Fasten one end of the hinge to the section you cut out and the other end to the door itself. You now have a door that will swing in and out when the dog pushes on it. Teach the dog how to use it by going in and out yourself a few times. *Make sure the neighbors aren't looking.*

Warning As a general rule, do not let anyone but *family members* use the dog's door without his permission. Small dogs easily get hurt feelings when they see strangers using their door.

Door for Large Dog If you have a very large dog, do not cut a section out of the door. Remove the door from the hinges it is now fastened to and replace them with new hinges that swing both ways. Attach these new hinges with Krazy Glue in precisely the same way you did the section you cut out if you had a small dog, only this time sideways.

The whole door will now swing in and out and your big dog will have no trouble. He won't even have to stoop.

Repairing Holes in Plaster Walls

Tools and Supplies Uncooked pizza (no sausage or cheese) or matzo meal, knife.

When you have holes in plaster walls either where pictures once hung or from some other form of abuse, they can be fixed in two easy ways.

If the wall is made of smooth plaster, have a pizza restaurant sell you a 12- or 14-in. pizza *uncooked, no sausage or cheese.* This is wonderful dough to work with and hardens well. Just take a wad of

dough, fill the hole and smooth off with a regular table knife. If, after you fill in all the holes, you still have some dough left over, you can make yourself a snack.

If your wall is the rough-finish plaster instead of the smooth, don't use pizza dough. Instead, get a box of matzo meal at a place that sells Kosher food. Following the directions on the box, make yourself several matzo balls about 6 in. around. This is a good size to work with, except for small holes. Follow the wadding and filling procedure described above, but do not use the knife. The matzo meal will dry rough instead of smooth and is perfect repair material for this kind of wall.

Notice These two repairs will work even if you are not Italian or Jewish.

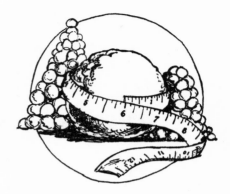

This is a self portrait of the artist. He should look so good.
—Editor

Inexpensive Sauna Conversion

Tools and Supplies Kitchen stove (new or old), 5-ft. camping tent, lots of aluminum wrap, stools, large kettle for chicken soup (optional).

It is not necessary to buy an expensive and professionally installed sauna when all you really want is a little heat on your body. You can have a sauna *in your kitchen* whenever you feel the urge and save truly extraordinary amounts of money if—and that's a big if—you will just pay attention this time.

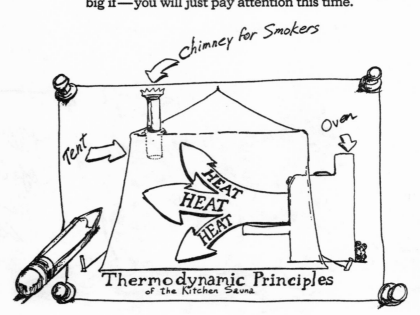

Thermodynamic Principles
of the Kitchen Sauna

Go to a sporting goods store and buy yourself a 5-ft. camping tent that has a large front opening. Bring it home and set it up in your kitchen right in front of the oven. Get yourself several small stools that you can place in the tent, so you and your friends can sit down and be comfortable. Cover the tent fabric with aluminum wrap or some other material that will make it difficult for the tent to "breathe." Now open the oven door and put the flap of the tent over the opening. When the oven is on, the heat will go right into the tent and stay there. Don't light the top burners.

To lose 5 lbs., set the oven control at 275° for 90 min. By adding 10° for another 10 min., you will lose another 5 lbs.

Eyehook in Ceiling (don't forget the drop of Crazy Glue)

5 Ft.

Explosion—
This is the best
the artist could do.
Now you see the
conditions of my
employment
—Editor

Warning The Surgeon General has determined that 400° for 4 hours is injurious to your health.

If you would rather have wet than dry heat, put a large kettle of chicken soup in the oven. Steam from chicken soup has been proven therapeutic.

Warning for Gas Stove Users If, after several minutes with oven set in the "on" position, you do not feel heat and are becoming a bit light-headed, *do not—I repeat—do not* light a cigarette.

Remove Door Handle
(this is the quick, noisy way)

Installing Sliding Doors in Place of Regular Kind That Open into a Room

Tools and Supplies Screwdriver, handsaw, string, eye-hooks, paste wax.

You will be delighted at how much more space you have when you put in doors that go into the wall instead of opening into the room and covering your walls.

Incredibly, for a home project of this type, you don't have to buy a thing except strings and eyehooks. First, remove the door han-

Door removed from Hinges

dles from both sides of the door. You do this because you are going to use the same door, only make it slide, and I assure you it won't go into the wall with the handles sticking out. Knock them off, with a sledge hammer if you must, but get them off the door. Now! Then remove the door from the doorway as you usually would. Do not fill the holes where the knobs were. We will use them later.

After the door is off its hinges, cut a hole with your metal coping saw the full length of the door in the wall that separates the two rooms. Do not cut the wall; that won't do any good at all. Be sure you are making the opening in the inside wall only. Otherwise, if it's an inside and outside wall, when you open the door, it will fall out into the yard, *taking you with it if you don't let go.*

After you have made a full-length opening, you will have to reach into the opening and saw out at least one of the 2x4's that are between the wall space into which the door is going to slide.

Fasten one eyehook in the door frame at the top on the left and one on the right. Connect a piece of string on each side of the door at the top and feed it through the hook. Of course use the standard crisscross stringing technique to get the door to slide in and out, in and out. If it slides up and down, either reverse the stringing or enjoy your portcullis. Now on the bottom of the door apply some

Top Left   *Top Right*

paste wax so it will slide well and slip easily into place. When you pull on the string on the right, the door will open. When you pull on the left string, the door will close. When you are out of the room where the strings hang, neither you nor anyone else can get back in again unless you (they) stick your (their) fingers in old holes.

Warning Do not attempt this installation if your walls are made of stone or cinder blocks.

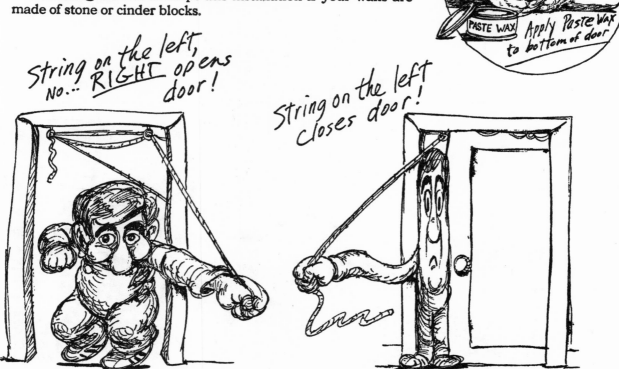

Apply Paste Wax to bottom of door

String on the left, No... RIGHT opens door!

String on the left closes door!

How to Fix Sagging Walls and Floors

Tools and Supplies Car jack, Krazy Glue, very sturdy rope, firecrackers or dynamite, unsuspecting stranger (optional), shovel, water, tea, coffee or other liquids, four trees all the same size.

If you find one end of your home is sinking, here's how to take care of it with little expense. You can also live in the house while you are doing the repairs, which will save you hotel bills.

First, dig hole under the corner of the house that is sinking. You can easily find the right corner by pouring water or other liquid on

Disturbed Gopher

Hole under Sinking Corner

your living-room floor and watching which way it runs. You may use coffee or tea but no coke, as coke will eat a hole in floor and create problems I have no interest in dealing with. If you have already used coke, contact the Nuclear Regulatory Commission for its brochure #372A, *Home Meltdowns and What to Do about Them*. Also, do not use prune juice, as it runs too fast to tell anything. The corner onto which the liquid runs is the one that is sinking and will from now on be called the "Naughty Corner."

With a shovel, start to dig a hole under the foundation of the Naughty Corner. If this goes too slowly, you might try a large firecracker, or even a little dynamite to loosen impacted dirt. It can be very dangerous if you decide to use dynamite, so see if you can get somebody else to do this part. After the hole is large enough so

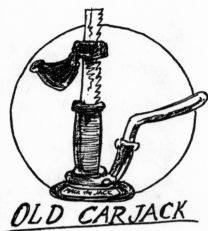

OLD CAR JACK

that you can slip an old car jack under the Naughty Corner of the house, do so. Now slowly, oh, ever so slowly, jack it up until the water on the living-room floor runs back to the center of the room.

Warning Remove the handle from the jack, so the nasty kids on your block don't let it down before you are ready.

Now, when the water stays in the center of the room, plant a full-grown, sturdy tree, perhaps a sequoia or dwarf redwood, as close as possible to the raised corner of the house and slip a section of rope under the raised Naughty Corner. Try to get a really heavy rope, if you can, the kind they use to tie ocean liners to the dock with, but a "good" clothesline will do in a pinch. Make a standard

Remove Jack Handle!!!
Kids may let it down, especially if you're under the house on inspection!!

House Haulers #7 sling/loop, slip the loop under the house and bring both ends up to a limb of the tree. Stretch the rope very tightly around a convenient branch and put one drop of Krazy Glue on the rope at the point where it touches the branch to keep it from slipping. It will hold up to 5,000 lbs. If you live in a two-story house, use two drops. As always, the good handyman thinks ahead. Why don't you try it, too? Plant four trees at the same time so if you want to work on more Naughty Corners, the trees will already be there waiting for you.

Caution: Redwoods aren't the best trees to use.

Warning Do not use this method on more than three corners of the house simultaneously. With four corners in a sling, the house will tend to sway. At least mine did.

Adding a Family Room to Your Home

Tools and Supplies See chapter on adding second floor. Eliminate the stepladder and yardstick. Add a power saw and insurance policy against self-mutilation.

Adding a room to your house need not be an intimidating job. If a sub-contractor, whom you will eventually call a dummy, can do it, you certainly can. If you can't, you're a bigger dummy than he is and wouldn't have been smart enough to buy this book.

If they did a satisfactory job, call the same crane company suggested in the chapter on roof repairs and rent the same two cranes with their operators. (Remember: Don't buy the cranes; they cost $150,000 each.) Have the cranes pick up your garage and set it down *touching* the wall of the house where you want to add a room. If the garage is very close to the house, rent a bulldozer instead of the cranes. (Do not buy the bulldozer; it costs $65,000.) Just have the garage pushed up against the wall of the house and stop making a federal case out of it.

After the garage is in place, you will have to put in a door to get from the house to the new room. Rent the kind of saw that is used for cutting down trees, so it will *go through both walls at once*, saving quite a bit of measuring time and guaranteeing that the hole will have a front and back. With shoddy labor, not all of them do these days.

It is not necessary to put up a door, as you will undoubtedly want to go in and out of the new room a lot. Since the foundation of

the garage did not move with the walls, the floor will be dirt, so be sure to put down plenty of scatter rugs. Scatter rugs give it a nice "sheik's tent" decor. For ventilation, you can open the garage door. Just as I said, it's so simple any dummy can do it.

Warning Don't clean dirt floor with water. *It turns to mud.* Don't vacuum dirt floor. Dirt floor goes up vacuum cleaners without stopping. Don't leave door open. Someone from force of habit might drive the car in. If this happens, build an adjoining garage.

For installing lights and plumbing, see other chapters. If you want to add a second floor, see next chapter. If the cranes or bulldozer are still hanging around, I'll bet you've run up a *big* bill.

Installing a Whirlpool in Your Bathtub

Tools and Supplies Tub of water, vacuum cleaner and hose.

If you are not a member of the jet set, you may not know how fantastically wonderful it is to take a tub bath that has a whirlpool in it. Because of the moving action of the water, you not only get much cleaner in a whirlpool tub, but you also come away relaxed

and stimulated at the same time. (Boy, do I like a whirlpool!) If you have ever sat in your washing machine (top loader model) when it was running, then you know the action I refer to.

Having a whirlpool installed can eat into your budget, particularly if you live on Social Security benefits, but with my system you can enjoy it as freely as you would a summer breeze. If you have only a shower stall in your bathroom and no tub, you'll have to get your kicks elsewhere, as you cannot whirlpool successfully in a shower stall.

First, fill your bathtub about half-full with water, but *don't get in yet*. Next, get your vacuum cleaner with the hose and bring it to the bathroom. You are going to do wonderful things in the water with it. Now, connect the hose to the blowing end (see chapter on unclogging drains).

Fill tub half way with water...

Vacuum Hose

Exhaust

...But don't get in!

45

Warning Make sure hose is *not* in the suction end of cleaner, or you will suck all the water out of the tub into one end of the vacuum and out the other, all over the rest of your house, like Hurricane Hilda.

With the cleaner running, place the loose end of the hose in the water. See all the wonderful bubbles and how fast the water churns? Don't just stand there looking at the dancing waters. Take off your clothes and get in! Pay no attention to the dust that might get into the water when you run the vacuum. A little dirt never killed anyone.

If you are careful you will not get electrocuted from this operation. Vacuum hoses are usually made of plastic or rubber and do not carry electricity. If you have a metal hose, borrow a vacuum with the right hose from your neighbor; otherwise, you'll kill yourself doing this — and who wants to be found dead and naked in the tub with the vacuum running? Even if you were voted the cleanest person at your Tupperware party, you wouldn't want them to think you vacuumed your bath water, would you?

Fireplace in Any Room

Tools and Supplies Bricks, yardstick, Krazy Glue, time.

There is hardly any room in a home that would not look better with a "designer" fireplace in it. It is so easy that even a simpleton can make one, so get going.

Buy at least 400 bricks because you'll want it high enough to put a mantel on. Decide on which wall you want the thing and just **start** by laying your bricks, *one on top of another,* against the wall, until it begins to look right. If you don't know when it looks right, ask someone with better taste than you have. To secure the structure, put a drop of Krazy Glue on each brick before you put it into **place.** Each brick should not weigh more than 5,000 lbs. Be sure to leave an opening right in the middle of the thing, or all you are doing is making a fancy brick wall in your room.

King Tut Fireplace

After the bricks are in place as high and as deep as you want them—stop. Now measure your fireplace and go out and buy a mantel at an antique shop. Be sure to get one that fits the size of the thing that you made. These can be quite expensive. A Louis XIV might cost more than your house, so shop wisely. After you lay the mantel in place over the brick fireplace, it should look just great.

Mt. Rushmore Memorial Fireplace

Figure this one out for yourself

Warning Whatever you do, don't try to light a fire in the fireplace. Remember, it's not a real one. If you had a real one, someone would have to build a chimney so the smoke could get out. I don't have a chapter on installing a whole chimney. You're on your own.

Installing Your Own TV Antenna

Tools and Supplies Five metal clothes hangers, broomstick, pliers, eyehook, TV antenna wire, Krazy Glue, used nylon stockings, aluminum foil or packages of Juicy Fruit gum, TV set with unsatisfactory reception.

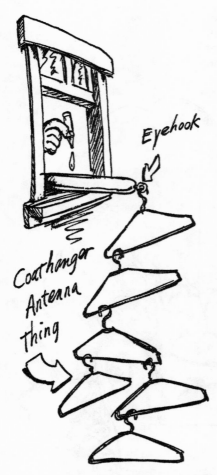

Eyehook

Coathanger Antenna thing

No need to buy an expensive TV antenna or hire an overpriced TV mechanic—whose mother wouldn't let him touch her set on a bet—when you can make and install one of your own. This will also save you from going out on the roof where you might get hurt. Your reception will be just as good as if you hired a man to jump around on your roof, making holes that will let in the rain or bats.

Take five metal clothes hangers from the closet (remove dry cleaners' cardboard for best results). Fold clothes that were on the hangers and put them away. Neatness is a virtue. Now get an old broomstick. From where? Just get it and quit asking questions. Connect all the hangers together by bending the hook part of each hanger tightly over any part of the other hangers with a pair of pliers. Leave the top hanger with the hook open. When you hold this thing up, it should look like an unattractive mobile.

Next, take the broom handle and screw in an eyehook at one end. Then take the hanger with the open hook and slip it through the eyehook in the end of the broomstick. When you hold it up, it should look like an unattractive mobile hanging from a broom handle.

Now take the end of your TV antenna wire and wrap it around any one of the hangers. It doesn't make any difference which hanger you wrap it around; it won't improve the T.V. shows. To get better shows, you have to write nasty letters to the networks and the FCC. Glue the wire that comes out of the back of your set to the hanger and put one drop of Krazy Glue on the end of the handle and stick it to your windowsill. One drop will hold up to 5,000 lbs. of hangers.

If you use five hangers, you get five channels. The more hangers you use, the more channels you get. If you want UHF, just hang a few pairs of old nylon stockings on several of the hangers and fill nylons with crumpled balls of aluminum foil or packages of Juicy Fruit gum.

Warning Once in place, do not put clothes on any of the hangers. This will eliminate the picture and all you'll get are radio announcements of pork belly futures and marine weather reports.

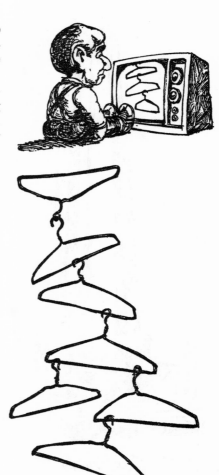

Roof Repairs Made Easy

Tools and Supplies Two construction cranes complete with operators, heavy-duty swimming-pool covers, Krazy Glue, plants.

For those of you who didn't follow my advice about installing a TV antenna and now find you have a leaky roofn here is a method that will fix the whole roof at one time instead of leak by leak.

Rent 2 Construction Cranes

As an emergency measure, until you can get the leaks stopped, place all your plants directly under the leaks. After leaks are fixed, you can put your plants back where they were and water them in your usual desultory fashion. Just why do you think they die all the time?

Because I don't like heights and I know a lot of you don't, I find it better to bring the roof down to me rather than me up to it.

You will need to rent two construction cranes, which stand about 10 stories high and move by diesel engines. Don't buy these, because you won't get that much additional use from them and they cost about $150,000 each. When you have them placed on

Dont be fooled by the artists inability to draw in proportion- The cranes are larger than the plants.
— Editor

←

I can Too!
— Artist

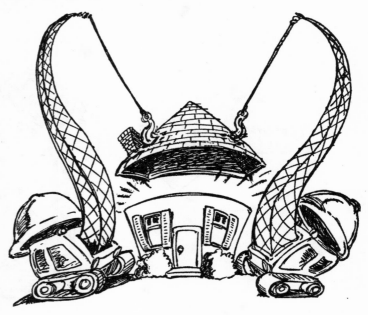

55

Trim off Excess

each side of your house, connect the long cables hanging from them under the eaves of your roof. Politely ask the two operators to lift the roof *at the same time and slowly lower it to the ground.*

After the roof is safely on the ground, do not begin repairs before you mark it front and back. If the swimming pool cover is not large enough to go over the openings in your roof, you will have to glue two together so they cover all the holes. A custom-made, swimming-pool roof cover is nice, but not necessary, and usually takes four to six weeks. Since the cranes are just sitting there wait-

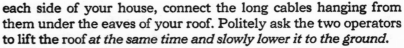

Stencil   "Front and Back"

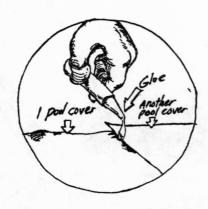

I pool cover   Gloe   Another pool cover

ing, they can lift the cover over the opening for you. Stretch the cover tight, being sure to leave a little hang over the sides all around. Trim off extra material.

Now have the cranes raise the roof and put it back in place, making sure they have not turned it around in the process. The weight of the roof will hold the plastic cover in place, and you will have a watertight house again. Not only that, but if it rains a lot, the space between the roof and the plastic cover will fill with water and you will have the only attic swimming pool on the block.

Notice cranes are more in proportion
— Artist

Plumbing-Unclogging for Apartment Dwellers Only

Tools and Supplies Hammer, vacuum cleaner with hose, tea with lemon.

Fixing stopped-up drains is a stomach-turning job which you should let someone else do, but, if you are too cheap to call in a professional, here's how you can do it yourself with a minimum of inconvenience.

At least 6 to 8 percent of the time, just by getting under the sink and hitting the pipes softly with a hammer, the sound will tell you just where the pipe is clogged, but since that won't help you in any way to get the glop out, don't bother.

The trouble usually comes about because of congestion from congealed grease, decaying vegetables, assorted gook that you should have put in the garbage, and hairballs. I told you it was disgusting—now I hope you'll believe me.

Instead of pouring that stuff down the drain, which will make your pipes mad at you forever, just get out your vacuum cleaner and put the hose *on the blowing end* of the machine instead of the sucking end. Put the loose end of the hose down the drain as far as it will reach.

Now, standing well clear, turn on the machine to its maximum power. With any luck the strong air pressure will blow all the dirt and garbage out of the pipe and into your neighbor's kitchen or bathroom.

Does this seem unfair to your neighbors? Nonsense. They will have exciting stories to tell about the day the garbage blew up on their ceilings and walls, more than compensating them for the inconvenience of cleaning their place up.

Warning Always do this operation while your neighbors are out because it's one thing to find garbage on your ceiling, it's another to see it exploding out of the drain.

To avoid the problem in the first place, treat your pipes in a humane way. Give them a little tea with lemon once a week. If you have a garbage disposal, be sure to give it a little roughage now and then.

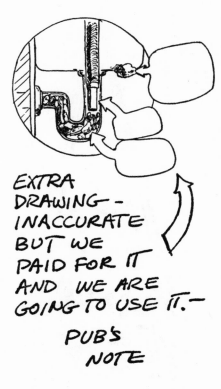

EXTRA
DRAWING—
INACCURATE
BUT WE
PAID FOR IT
AND WE ARE
GOING TO USE IT.—

PUB'S
NOTE

Repairing Toilet Bowl

Tools and Supplies Eyehooks, hand drill, 20-ft. string, Krazy Glue, stepladder (or tiptoes).

If your toilet will not flush because the little handle won't pull up the stopper in the bottom of the tank, you can fix it without spending more than a few dollars and have some fun in the bathroom while you are at it.

First, standing on a small stepladder—or, if you are very tall, on your tiptoes—with the hand drill, make a small hole in the ceiling directly over the toilet. Place a drop of Krazy Glue on the eyehook, screw it into the hole in the ceiling. (That was your first bit of fun.) The Krazy Glue makes the eyehook secure and holds up to 5,000 lbs. Next, take the top off your toilet water tank and place it wherever you keep your other spare toilet tank tops. You won't need it anymore, but you can make a wonderful planter or wet bar out of this top. (Personally, I like a planter better, and you can get full directions for this conversion in the chapter on toilet planters, which will appear in my next book, tentatively scheduled for publication in 1987.)

Flush the toilet and, before the water rises and you get your hands wet, tie one end of the string through the end of the rubber stopper in the bottom of the tank using a standard plumber's underwater ascot knot with a Rickover tie-off. Feed the other end of the string through the eyehook in the ceiling and let it drop on the floor next to the toilet seat.

Take handle off tank, since you won't need it anymore up there, and tie the end of string through the hole in the end of it or simply to it if no hole seems to be there. You now have something perfect to pull on the string with. When you want to flush, you just pull on the handle which will, in turn, pull on the string and raise the rubber stopper at the bottom of the tank. Congratulations! Don't forget to let go of the handle after it flushes, so the stopper will fall, thus stopping the water. If, because you botched something in these instructions, the toilet will not stop flushing, you can overcome the problem by tying another piece of string around the rod connected to the big ball float that is supposed to rise to the top of the tank to stop the water from running. You may use the same eyehook. Put loose end through the eyehook and let it fall next to the one with the handle on it. Now for some more fun. Put an eyehook in the wall close to the toilet. After you have flushed, when you want the water to stop, just pull the string 'til the ball is at the top of the tank and wrap it around the hook to hold it in place.

A little practice and you will be an expert toilet flusher. *All this is best done from a sitting position.*

Warning If mechanical problems persist, cut down on liquids and whole grain foods and spend lots of time visiting friends or relatives.

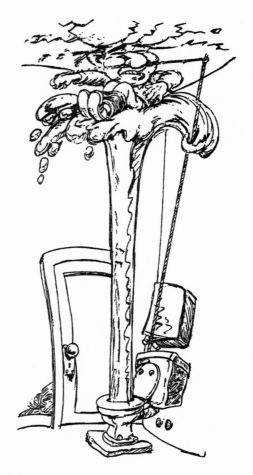

Installing a Peephole
in Your Door

Tools and Supplies Large door, good wood saw, one-way see-through glass, one live person for head size, smaller people with heads if you can get them.

I certainly don't want to be an alarmist. There are enough people creating a climate of fear and distrust without my adding to it with sharp observations about the growth of violent crime

everywhere you look. But I can tell you one thing—never open your front door unless you know for sure who's there. But if you want to know who is there without opening the door, it can be done very easily. It's just not safe anymore to open the door for just anybody who rings your chimes.

Have the member of your family *with the biggest head* stand next to the door and see where his head comes to. I use the head, because that usually tells you more about who is at the door than do knees. Looking at someone's navel does not tell you much either, unless it's nude and you really know the person well, or have marked his or her navel in some way.

With a pencil, make a circle on the door about the size of a person's head and at the height you measured with your live family member. Now, get several people of different heights to stand next to the door, so you can draw the outline of their heads, also. This will give you a good cross section of the types of people you expect to be looking at through your safety-viewing hole. Don't forget the children, as they can be particularly dangerous when they come ringing the bell.

Now with your saw, cut around each outline of head starting at the top of the door and going down as low as necessary. You should now have a good clean hole to look through at different places in your door. For the really small kids, you may find you have holes 3 ft. from the bottom, but that's all right. It will help you to identify visiting midgets and dogs. Unfortunately, you will not be able to see mice, frogs, birds (unless in flight) or turtles, but in some areas this will not be a problem.

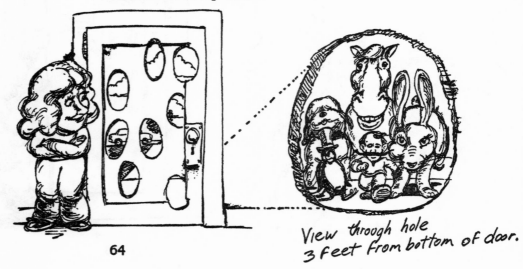

View through hole 3 feet from bottom of door.

To complete your safety-viewing hole, install the one-way glass. You can get it at your hardware store. (It is much cheaper to buy it already made than to make your own. You would need a great deal of sand.) After you have had the glass cut a tiny bit larger than the hole, install it by pushing it into the hole with your feet. This is called the friction method.

Warning In forcing glass into hole with feet, remove shoes first so glass does not break.

Warning Remember, the glass only "sees" from one side and is a mirror on the back side. If you should see a reflection of yourself in glass as you are approaching to answer the door, then you put it in backwards. Why you would do a thing like that—after all the trouble you went to—is something I'll never figure out, so why should I bother trying?

Two Way Glass

Outside Burglar Alarm

Tools and Supplies, etc. Heavy black thread, lots of wooden sticks, big drill, record player with outside speakers, recording of Beethoven's *Fifth*, an intruder.

Now that you have made a number of my suggested improvements to your home and have invested in a substantial amount of tools and supplies, you should get a burglar alarm system that will help protect them. Tools and supplies have been

prime targets for burglars, because they have lots of spare time during the daylight hours, are often good with their hands, and are into doing things for themselves. Don't buy a "sophisticated" electronic system as they know what makes it operate, and you can't fool them one bit. Putting up a metal plate in your yard, or decals on your windows, as a warning that your home is protected by an alarm system no longer fools today's burglars. They are known to make a collection of these plates. But there is a very inexpensive, deceptively simple, system called "The Trip System" that always works.

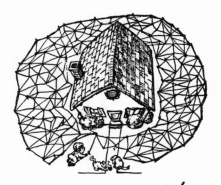

Artist—
These look like
spider webs to me.
—Editor

Editor—
Wrong again.
—Artist

About 2 ft. from your house, in the yard, set up some small wooden stakes about 5 ft. apart, so that they stick out of the ground *no more than 3 in.* They can be made of any kind of wood and do not have to be all the same, but they should be painted black. Into the top of each screw a small eyehook so that it's secure.

Run a nice strong black thread through the eyehooks and completely around the outside of the house, until the house is enclosed like a fly caught in a spider's web. Drill a hole in the wall of the room that has your record player in it, pull the thread from the outside through the wall, and tie it to the off/on switch on your record player which should have the volume control turned up high.

Thumb of a True Handyman

Eyehook Top of Stick

drill Hole

Before you go to bed, make sure the record is in place on the turntable. If anyone comes within two feet of your house, he will trip over the invisible thread, starting the record player, which will be waiting for him at full volume. Here's where the fun really begins. Can you imagine Beethoven's *Fifth* at full volume? Gosh, a burglar will be surprised and shocked unless, of course, he is an unemployed, classically trained musician. This will surely scare off all but a very better class of crook, as studies indicate they do not, in general, dig classical music.

If you want to get fancy, for a few extra dollars you can install a set of outside speakers. There won't be anyone for blocks around that won't hear your record player, and they'll call the police. (Studies show that most neighbors don't like classical music and will be glad to call the police just to stop Beethoven.)

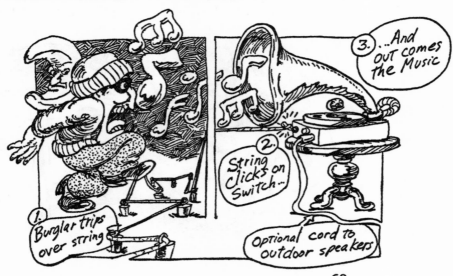

Dripping Faucet Repair

Tools and Supplies Package of assorted corks, small hammer, small pliers, corkscrew, strong wrist, philosophical attitude.

If you have a dripping faucet, it is easy to stop it without a plumber. You can turn off the water valve under your sink, but that means you must get down on the floor each time to turn the faucet on and off. If this doesn't strike you as terribly inconvenient, there's something terribly wrong with your judgment and I can't fix that.

For a cost of less than $2, you can get yourself a package of assorted corks at a hardware store. Find one just the right size for your faucet opening. You will have about ten to choose from, so one will always fit. If not, stop reading and go back to turning the

valve under the sink. Things are tough all over. If you find one that does fit to stop the dripping, all you have to do is push the cork into the mouth of the faucet as far as you can by hand. Then hit it with a small hammer, driving it in until it is *very tight.*

Caution I hope you were smart enough to leave a small amount of the cork sticking out of the faucet. If not and you hammered the cork too far into the faucet, use a common corkscrew to remove it. For gosh sakes, be more careful next time.

When you want to use the water, you just take a small pair of pliers and pull the cork out. When you are finished with the water, you replace the cork the same way you put it in originally.

Caution If water pressure builds up behind the cork and blows it out, apply one drop of Krazy Glue and hammer it back in. Krazy Glue will hold up to 5,000 lbs. of water pressure.

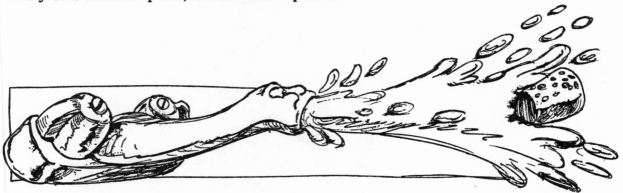

De-Sooting and Cleaning House Chimney

Tools and Supplies Six Santa Claus suits, 6 silly neighborhood kids, 1 ladder reaching roof.

I tell you it isn't Dick Van Dyke singing "Bibbidi Bobbidi Boo" when you have to clean your own filthy chimney. You are in for dirty work if your fireplace is not breathing well and soot pours into your living room every time you use it. But there are ways that the resourceful do-it-yourselfer can deal with the problem,

save lots of money, and have a wickedly amusing afternoon. Here's how:

Buy (do not rent, the store will not take them back) inexpensive Santa Claus suits. Next, without drawing undo attention to yourself, get six of the smallest kids in your neighborhood who can walk and tell them that your house has been selected by the North Pole Association to have the Santa Claus helper tryouts.

Now get the kids dressed in their suits (help if you must) and spray just enough water on them to *make each suit a little damp.* Then have each kid climb a ladder to the roof, get into the chimney, and *fall straight down.* As each one comes through, he will

bring a large amount of soot with him and a lot will also cling to his damp body.

Send each kid through about six times, no matter how he looks or protests. Quitters aren't winners. Tell the kids Santa Claus is watching, and by Christmas (or Chanukah) he will decide on his official assistant. Six times for each should give you a good clean chimney, and all it cost was six Santa Claus outfits and maybe a little coaxing.

Warning Make sure andirons have been removed and fire in fireplace is out before a kid starts his fall.

If a kid gets stuck in the chimney, *follow immediately with a heavier kid*. If that does not work, see chapter on clogged drains.

This procedure may make your living room a little dirtier than usual so when the maid comes to clean, tell her she missed a lot last time. If you are going to do the room cleaning yourself, have the kids climb up a ladder placed *in* the chimney so they can deposit the soot on the roof where it can blow onto your lawn and provide healthful fertilizer. If you select the second method you must have a second ladder outside the house so the kids can get down off the roof.

Putting in New Lock on Front or Back Door

Tools and Supplies New locks, Krazy Glue, drill.

No matter where you live nowadays, safety demands that the doors on your house or apartment can be locked so that you feel secure when you are away from home. Even if you never leave your home, you should always keep your door locked to all strangers, most relatives, and some friends.

There are many different type locks available on the market today. Some use a key and are called "key locks." Others use a combination of numbers and are called "combination locks." Get this complex terminology right or you will look like a fool at the hardware store, where your reputation is already not so great.

For real security, I suggest putting one of each on the same door. No burglar— even if he has a gold-plated set of keys to your dump— is going to stand around and figure out your combination. If he has the combination but doesn't have the key to fit your key lock, he may be so disappointed he'll leave. If he has both combination and key, you don't deserve to have a secure home.

Let's first replace the old key lock. You can remove the old lock from the door by hitting it real hard on one side with a sledge hammer, forcing it through the door and out the other side, or you

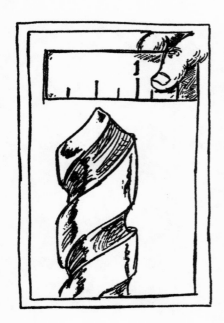

can simply undo the ring washer that holds it in place and easily slip it out the other side. This method is better because it is less noisy and messy than the hammering procedure. (I hope you read both techniques before using the sledge hammer.) Once the old lock is out of the hole, the new lock should slip right into the place where the old one was.

To add the combination lock, you will need to drill a new hole in the door somewhere above the old one. Don't go too high. You want to be able to reach it conveniently when you are opening the lock. For once in your life, follow the directions on the box the combination lock comes in. After you have the hole in the door, if lock does not slip into place, put it in as far as it will go and bang the door up against the wall behind it. Constant, hard banging will force the lock the rest of the way into the hole. (See chapter on wall repair.)

Warning Make sure you install the new combination lock with the combination knob on the outside of the house, otherwise you will have to work the combination to get out instead of in. This might make leaving the house more trouble than it's worth.

Suggestion If you can't memorize the combination, you can tack it on the door next to the lock, but *do it in a foreign language*. (Chinese or Latin would be best since tests prove that there are few burglars that speak or understand these languages.)

And remember, even if you forget your key and combination, you can always go in and out through an open window. Do not let anyone know about the open window.

Spray Painting Walls or Furniture or Things

Tools and Supplies Paint, vacuum cleaner with spray-gun attachment, gas or oxygen mask, exhaust fan, furniture covers, overalls or surgical gown, rubber gloves.

Are you familiar with the cost of professional painters these days and how sloppy they can be? Not only that, but they are often critical of your taste and color choices. Who needs them? Why

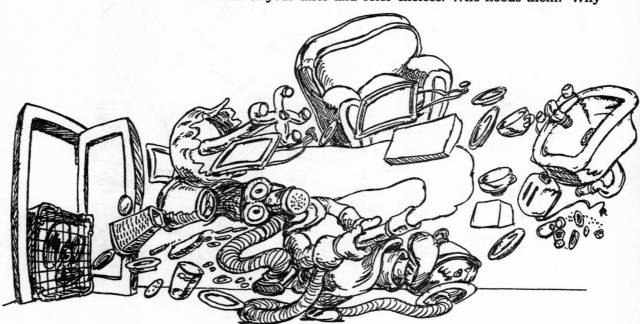

should you subject yourself to such treatment and humiliation? Do it yourself and *keep the humiliation in the family.*

In painting the walls of a room, or even furniture, it is much easier to do it by spraying than with a brush or roller. You have no streak marks to cover up.

First, get the color of paint you want to use; then get out your vacuum cleaner. Yes, your vacuum cleaner. What did you expect — a toaster? Just connect the hose to the blowing end and you

Keep turpentine soaked rag around for at least a year.

have a spray gun. Be sure the hose is on the blowing end of the cleaner. If it is on the sucking end by mistake, all your paint will be sucked into the vacuum, and that won't do any good, unless you want to paint the inside of your vacuum.

Rent the biggest exhaust fan you can find and stand it in front of an open door or window to take out the overspray (as we say). You are almost ready to begin. Get all the extra sheets you have in the house and *cover everything that you don't want painted.* Now, you are ready.

Start the fan. Put on your overalls or surgical gown, rubber gloves, and either a gas or oxygen mask. Both have built-in goggles so you can see what you are doing. Start the vacuum and hold the spray gun about 1 ft. from the surface you are hoping to paint. The paint will come from the gun in a fine spray, will go on very easily, and you will be done in no time.

If any paint gets on your goggles or oxygen mask, use a turpentine rag to get it off before it dries and you can no longer see what you are doing. (Keep the turpentine rag moist for one year because you will be finding paint overspray for a long time.)

Note For excessive paint-overspray repair, see chapter on wallpapering.

Glass Replacement in Windows

Tools and Supplies New glass, tape measure, putty knife, clear roll of plastic sheet, Krazy Glue, pasta dough.

Some jobs seem much more complex than they are. Some seem much simpler than they turn out to be. Fixing a broken window may be one or the other or neither. But enough of philosophy; on to repairs.

First you must remove the piece of broken glass. As it is very hard to do this part of the job without cutting your hands on the jagged edges, see if you can get someone else to do it. When the frame is clear of broken glass and the dried putty that held the glass in frame, measure the opening to determine the size the new glass will have to be. Measure it again. If the two measurements are the same, you're in good shape. If they are not, try to find out

STEP RIGHT UP

REMOVE THE BROKEN GLASS And win a box of BANDAIDS

what stupid mistake you made. Keep trying until you get two consecutive similar measurements.

Go to a hardware store with your measurements and have a new piece cut to that size. (You could make your own glass, but the sand will absolutely ruin your oven.) Do not try to get glass at the grocery store. They're usually out of stock on it except for their own windows, which they will not give you no matter how good a customer you are.

After you get your new glass home — and if you haven't already broken it through careless handling — call the same pizza place that you used when you filled the hole in your wall and have them deliver a large, uncooked pizza — again no sausage or cheese. Work dough up well in your hands till it is pliable, then break off a small piece. Holding the new glass in place with one hand, spread pizza around the frame where you scraped off the dried putty. In one hour the dough will be dry and glass will stay in place. If you are in a hurry to go out, you can use your hair dryer for quicker drying.

Warning The pizza dough may make everyone on the outside look a bit Italian. This is only a temporary effect.

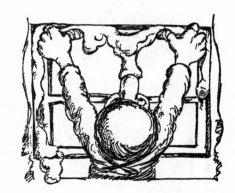

An even less expensive way to repair your window is to cut a piece of clear plastic from the roll so that it is just the right size to go across your window frame, put a drop of Krazy Glue in each corner and press it against the frame. With four drops on the frame, you are protected up to 20,000 lbs. of wind velocity. A direct blow from a tornado might tear it a little.

Suggestion Next time listen to your mother and don't play baseball in the house.

Installing Your Own Central Heating System

Tools and Supplies 100 ft. of flexible dryer hose, several electric fans (8 in.), Krazy Glue, kitchen oven.

In case you haven't noticed, we live in a fuel-short society. Doubling up on our resources is not only patriotic, but also shows that *American Know How* did not die with Leonardo Da Vinci, Baron von Hindenburg and Marconi.

Buy 100 ft. of the kind of flexible hose you use on your clothes dryer to exahust it out the window. For a better buy, keep in mind that it also comes in 10,000-ft. rolls, but, unless you live in the Taj

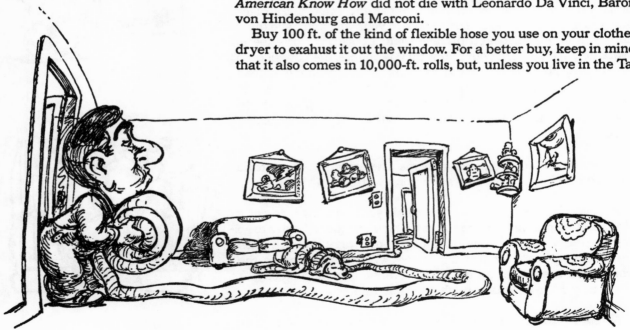

Mahal, you are going to have a lot left over. If you have a 6-room house, get 6 small (8-in.) electric fans. Starting in your kitchen, measure the exact number of feet from the oven to the door of each room in the house that you wish to heat. Cut the hose into pieces just the right length to reach from the oven door to the rooms.

Open the oven door, and with one drop of Krazy Glue cement the hose segments to the inside of the open door and unroll hose from oven door to rooms to be heated. If you are heating 6 rooms, you will have 6 hoses stretched, *as inconspicuously as possible,* to the various rooms. If you are heating a room on the second floor, drill a hole the exact diameter of the hose in the floor of the second-floor room to be heated, and lift hose through the hole for direct heating. Happily, hot air rises.

In front of each end of hose in each room to be heated, place one of the fans and connect it to the nearest electric plug. It won't work if you don't plug it in.

Turn on the oven and allow it to get warm. Turn on the fan in each room to be heated. The fan will suck the hot air from the oven to each room, letting you control the temperature of the rooms. If one room gets too hot, just turn off the fan in that room.

Hot air rises and is blown into room by fan.

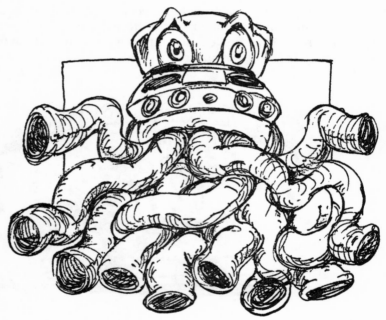

Warning To avoid tripping over hoses or hitting your head on hoses that go to the second floor, paint the hoses in bright, decorator colors. The overall effect is not only practical and stunning and can smell terrific. The aromas from the oven will be carried to every room of your house, so be sure you bake only the foods you really enjoy. Cake smells best.

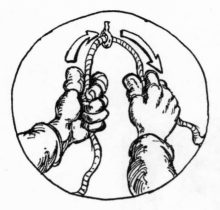

Repairing an Oscillating Electric Fan

Tools and Supplies String, eyehooks, two people, two chairs, cooperative attitude.

The first thing to go bad with an oscillating electric fan is the thing that makes it oscillate. This is a funny-looking group of gears that fits somewhere in the back of the fan and hangs down like a growth on the outside. When the gears break a tooth, it throws the whole oscillating mechanism off, so the fan just sits there and cools one person — if that person happens to be in front of it. If no one is in front of it, it cools nobody. If you had only wanted to cool one person, you wouldn't have bought an oscillating fan in the first place, so, from where I look at it, without my fix-it advice you're in big trouble.

2 FT.

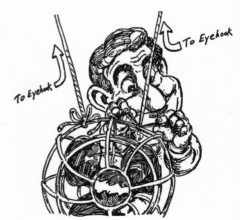

To Eyehook

To Eyehook

There's no need to take the broken fan to an expensive fan-repairing shop when all you will need to get it moving again is a long piece of string, two eyehooks, and two people in two chairs in different places.

Here's how. Place the fan on a table in the middle of your room and install eyehooks in the ceiling on each side of your fan about 2 ft. out from the fan's frame. Thread the string through the eyehooks, tie it around the fan guard, one on each side. Bring the ends over to the chair where someone sits. If there is no one sitting there, get someone, or this repair won't work and you'll have eyehooks in the ceiling for no purpose, which is dumb.

Now when you turn on the fan and want it to oscillate, have the people sitting in the chairs pull on the strings, thus causing the fan to turn and blow in their direction.

Warning *Only one person pulls at a time,* or else the fan does not know which way to turn and will fall off the table, breaking something more important than the oscillating device.

Landscaping Your House and Property

Tools and Supplies Trees from several areas, construction crane, steam shovel, swan and other water-type birds, 2x4's, pride. Optional—deer and antelope.

Landscaping your property is a matter of taste, so you would do a lot better to depend on mine than to go out and do things on your own. Most people plant the same tired bushes and shrubs because they are followers, not leaders. In the landscape biz they are called "lookalikes." If you just want to be a lookalike, stop where you are. If you want your house to be the showplace of your neighborhood, read on.

If you are reading this sentence, congratulations. Those lookalikers aren't very imaginative, and in my opinion they smell funny, too.

I assume your house is sitting on a lot at least 200 ft. x 200 ft. and you have plenty of space to give your home an appropriate "estate" look. First, purchase two California redwoods. You can buy them in the northern part of California, and they can be brought to your area by railroad car. Air freight companies do not fly them because they are larger than their planes. You can also have them delivered by flatbed truck if your private railroad siding is being redecorated.

After the trees are in your yard, rent a large construction crane. The rental agent can also supply a steam shovel that you will need to dig a hole at least 12 ft. deep to hold the roots. Do not dismiss either the crane or the shovel. You will need them a bit later and as a person of obvious substance, you can afford to have them hanging around.

Have the crane set the tree into place and the tractor push the dirt into the hole so that the tree stands straight. You may have to hold it up for a few years with 2x4's until it gets its footing back.

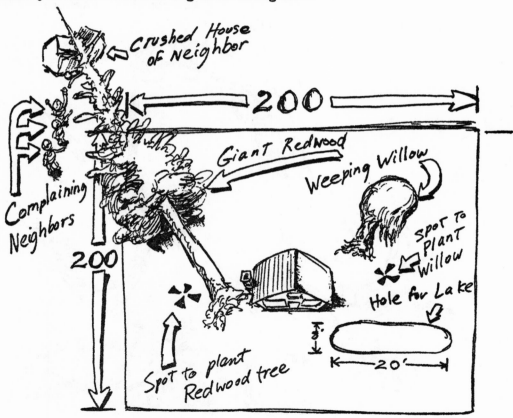

The tree should have been planted on the left of the house **as you** face it. If you planted it on the right, have the tractor turn your house so that it faces the other way.

On the right side (or the left—depending on which **way your** house is now facing), have the steam shovel dig a hole deep enough for the weeping willow you should have ordered from a southern tree supply company.

When the crane has set the weeping willow into its hole, have the tractor dig still another hole, this one near the willow, about 8 ft. deep and at least 20 ft. long. The exact shape makes no real difference, because this will be the lake that the swans and other water birds you ordered will swim in. (You may wish to use the shape of your family crest as a guideline.) Fill the lake with Perrier water and bring your swan and other water-loving birds home.

Suggestion For the redwood side of the house have a few deer and antelope on the grounds. It will give that area a real woodsy look.

Warning If you are afraid that the animals will wander off your grounds, place a leash on everything that can get away, even the swan — or hire a brace of gamekeepers.

Wallpapering

Tools and Supplies Putty knife, small stepladder, water hose, mop, electric iron, gravity, pair of rubbers for your feet.

Nothing brightens up a room like good-looking wallpaper and *it is so easy to put up.* No need to call in the paperhangers to mess up your house with their dirty tarpaulins and tools. You can do that all by yourself and have undreamed-of new experiences in the satisfying world of do-it-yourself.

If you want a real good-looking wall when you are finished, you'll have to remove the old wallpaper. You may use either of my removal methods. Neither one is really all that good, but there are no really good ways to get rid of old wallpaper and I'm doing the best I can.

First, scrape the old stuff off. To do this you need a putty knife. Once you get a little section started, you can pull and either (1) the paper will come off, or (2) a section of the wall will come down. If a section of the wall comes out, before you proceed, *put it back*. (See chapter on filling in wall holes— matzo balls or pizza.) Pulling

from the top to the floor is the easiest way to utilize the scraping method, because it takes advantage of gravity (if you have any in your area).

A second procedure is to steam the old paper off the walls, but this usually means renting a wall steamer, which makes a lot of mess. You can accomplish the same thing — and save money — by wetting down your wall with a hose until the paper is *very well saturated.* Try not to get more water on the floor than you need. (If all the water runs to one side of the room, see chapter on raising sinking floors.)

When the walls are thoroughly wet, get out your electric iron. When it's good and hot, place the flat side of the iron on the wallpaper, just as you would on your clothes. Steam forms at once

when the hot iron touches the very wet paper. By using the step-ladder, you can iron the whole wall and the paper will get so loose, you can just peel it right off.

Caution Throughout both operations, work as carefully as you can. Many great murals by old masters have been found hiding under wallpaper. Check your wall carefully before putting up new paper. (You may disregard this advice if you live in Hoboken.)

Artist—
No reference
to this art.
—Editor

Editor—
There was
before you cut
the copy.
—Artist

More Tools and Supplies Now that you have the paper off the wall, here's what you will need to put the new paper on: ladder, flour and water, bucket, paper, brush, electric steam iron, yardstick, card or coffee table, scissors, wallpaper, thumbtacks, old paintbrush.

As I said, this whole thing is a snap— now comes the fun.

Spread the wallpaper face down on your card or coffee table. Measure the wall from ceiling to floor with a yardstick and don't make any mistakes, because once you cut the paper, *that's it*. Measure it again. Funny how walls change size up close.

You can make your own wallpaper paste out of the flour and water and save even more money. Use two parts flour to one part water, give or take a little depending on the lumps. *Try for no lumps;* it makes for a smoother wall.

Warning Don't use Bisquick for your flour; it has a tendency to rise after the paper is on the wall. This is permissible only if your paper has biscuits in the pattern.

*Artist —
I don't get it.
— Editor*

*Editor —
What's the matter with you? It's a dog defending his master from attacking wallpaper!
— Artist*

*Artist —
Oh.
— Editor*

After paste is ready, spread it on paper with paintbrush, making absolutely sure the pattern side of the paper is *face down*. This may seem incredibly elementary to you, but, if someone had told me about that trick the first time I papered, it would have saved me hours of getting the paste off the pattern.

After your paste is on the back of the paper, run as fast as you can up your ladder and get the paper on the wall. Don't let anything get in your way during these critical seconds.

Have your thumbtacks ready, because if the paste dries on the paper before you get it on the wall, the paper will fall off the wall in no time — even before you have a chance to get your steam iron hot again. Press the wall with the iron. The steam will soften and dry the paste and the paper will stick to the wall beautifully. When it dries fully, it will be easier to take the wall down than remove the paper.

If you can't get the paper and paste to hold even after ironing, you can keep the paper up with the thumbtacks — but this *does not look professional*. You could also call in a wallpaper man, but make sure he brings his own paste, thumbtacks, and iron.

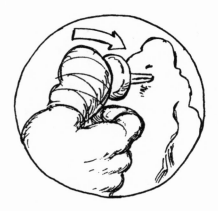

Warning If you are afraid your first attempt won't look too good, start in your neighbor's home or apartment, after making sure he's away on vacation. When you feel you have it down pat, tackle your own place.

Suggestion Leftover paste put in a 350° oven for one hour makes wonderful Lebanese bread and has little caloric content.

NOTE! This bread m made from Wallpaper Paste

Making Inside Garage Out of Little-Used Family Room

Tools and Supplies Three 2x4's, an extra 2x4, Krazy Glue, garage door with an automatic opening device, string charge from army surplus, no-fault insurance policy.

We have all seen the advertisements in TV magazines for inexpensive garages. If it's easy for them, with your intelligence, natural grace, charm and good looks it will be a snap.

Determine where the door is going to hang on the outside of your house by locating the old family room from the outside. If you

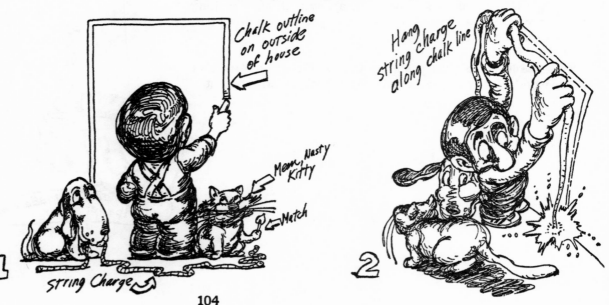

Chalk outline on outside of house

Mean, Nasty Kitty

Match

1   string Charge

Hang string charge along chalk line

2

have any doubts, ask someone more intelligent than you. With white chalk, outline on the outside wall where the opening of the new door is to be. If you set your charge right, the hole should be pretty close to the place you want it. If you do this incorrectly, the hole could be on the wrong side of the house, so locating the old family room from the outside is an important step, probably the most important. To make the opening just the right size, hang the string charge along the chalked line you have marked. Use the same type of charge the army sappers do. It can be purchased in any army surplus store in most mining towns in South Africa, and in South America and a few select Mafia-controlled outlets in the United States.

Warning Do not hammer or staple string charge to wall. A little of the Krazy Glue will hold it in place until you are ready. Igniting the charge can be dangerous, so if possible ask someone dumber than you to actually set it off.

Set off the charge?
Are you okay?
You will use the 2x4's to make a frame for the hole you made in the wall. If the house looks like it might collapse, use some of the 2x4's to hold it up. Glue the frame together, and when it is dry, force it into the opening you have made. If there is extra space around the frame, fill it in with old newspapers.

If there is extra space around the frame, STUFF IT with old newspapers.

DAILY NOOZ
TITANIC SINX

DAILY NOOZ

Install the door-opening mechanism, *according to the manufacturer's directions,* to the ceiling of the family room. Use Krazy Glue to hold it. One drop will hold a door up to 5,000 lbs.

Attach the door to the opening mechanism. Press the remote control button. The door should go up and down. *If the house goes up and down, you have done something wrong.* If the door cycles will not stop, either wedge the extra 2x4 under the door to hold in open position, or practice getting your car in and out while the door is on the way up.

Caution Do not have dents removed from car until you have your timing in and out just right.

Adding Second Floor to a One-Story Flat-Roof House

Tools and Supplies One-story house, garage, 2 construction cranes, 8-ft. stepladder, yardstick, saw, Krazy Glue.

To add a second story to your house, you must have a free-standing garage and a house with a flat roof. A pitched-roof house with a garage on top is both unsafe and ugly.

Measure your house roof with a yardstick to see how wide it **is**. Then do the same with the floor of your garage. They don't **have** to be the same but close.

Rent (don't buy, because they cost $150,000 each) two construction cranes with operators. Have each crane fasten its cable to each end of the garage. Slowly lift it and set it down on the roof of your house. That was the hard part, and you didn't do a lick of work except to make out a check to the crane rental company.

Artist's Mother loves these construction cranes. Who am I to argue with a nearsighted old lady? — Editor

Warning Car must be removed from garage prior to placing your garage on roof. If you didn't remove the car, call the cranes back, have them lower the garage to the ground, remove the car, and put the garage back on the roof where they found it.

The roof of the house has now become the floor of the second story. Decide where you want the stairway, and with a good saw, from the second floor, cut a 5-ft.-square opening in the roof. Put an

8-ft. stepladder under the hole in the roof, and you have a comparatively perfect stairway. Watch the top step, it's a little tricky.

Oh, yes, before the garage is put down on the roof, squeeze two drops of Krazy Glue on each corner of the house roof. That will hold the garage to the roof in winds up to 5,000 miles an hour. Since one drop of glue will hold up to 5,000 lbs., be sure to weigh your garage to determine whether it will need one or two drops of Krazy Glue.

Installing Electric Outlets in Room

Tools and Supplies Krazy Glue, small pictures, hammer and chisel, wall socket, electric drill, several feet of electric wire, plain pizza—no tomato, no cheese, hold the sausage—matzo meal, artistic sense, intuition.

I know it's hard to believe, but you don't need to call in an expensive electrician just to install a new wall socket in your room.

(This is a fairly straightforward job requiring little more than patience, an artistic temperament, and a willingness to risk one's life for the accolade of "a job well done.") Just follow these simple directions.

First, assemble in the room in which you want the new socket all the appliances that you ever plug in—the vacuum cleaner, TV set, fans, lamps, radio, iron, shaver, toaster, typewriter, mixer, vibrator, blender, and anything else that I have forgotten. See how much cord each has and decide where would be the best place to put the new socket. Don't pay unnecessary attention to tradition. I always put my sockets at eye level so I don't have to stoop when plugging in and outplugging. Of course, if you are over 5'8" only other tall people will be able to use an eye-level socket easily, so you will have to decide what's right for you.

Now find the electric wire that is already in the wall so you can tap into it with your new wire. You can locate the electric wire by punching holes in the wall with your hammer and chisel, wherever

Outside Insulation

Inside, but still Outside Insulation

Wire

your intuition tells you the wire might be. If your family is home, you can make a game out of finding the wire by giving all those over six years of age a hammer and chisel and letting them use their intuition, too. The one with the best intuition will probably get a shock. *Don't worry about the extra holes in the wall.* I will tell you how to use them later.

Now measure out the number of feet of new wire you will need to go from where you found the original wire in the wall to where you want the new outlet. You won't have to turn off the electricity unless you plan to touch both wires at the same time. From the length of wire you have cut, scrape off one-half inch of the insulation so you can see the wire underneath. Do the same thing to the wire in the wall. One wire at a time, please. Remember, the current is still on. Take the ends of the wire you cut and wrap them around the wire you have exposed in the wall. Put a drop of Krazy Glue on the connection and in a few seconds it will be tight. The glue will hold up to 5,000 volts.

Next, chisel out the plaster in the wall and make a kind of shallow trench from where you made the connection to where you want the new outlet. Try to take the shortest route possible across your wall. If you have some string in the house, you can cut a piece to reach from Point A to Point B and hold it in place with thumbtacks.

After you have finished trenchingn make a hole with your electric drill in the wall where the new socket is going. (Now you know why we didn't turn the current off.) Lay the wire in the wall trench and connect the loose wire ends, *one at a time,* to the screws on the socket. Push the socket into the wall and put the face-plate back on the front of the socket. To save screws, put some Krazy Glue on the back of the face-plate to hold the whole thing into the wall. The glue holds sockets up to 5,000 lbs.

114

To fix the wall trench, see my chapter on plastering walls. Depending on the kind of finish you want, order either the pizza dough or the matzo balls. As for the holes you made in the wall, put pictures over them and make a nice wall gallery. No one will know the difference and they will think you have quite an eye for art. Use the Krazy Glue to hang the pictures. Krazy Glue will hold pictures up to 5,000 lbs.

Pop-Up Toaster Repair

Tools and Supplies Eyehooks, pop-up toaster, bread for toast, glass of water, fishhook (small), Krazy Glue, string, window-shade pull handle.

When small appliances get out of order, you don't have to take them to expensive repair shops where chances are they don't know any more about fixing them than you. For example, here's what to do if your toaster is broken. (If your toaster is working or if you don't have a toaster, don't read this chapter. Or read it and fill your head with useless information. See if I care.)

The most common trouble with the automatic toaster is that it stops being automatic and will not pop the toast out — even if you yell nasty things at it in German. This is usually due to the spring timing on the bottom having gone awry (or deafness). If it's the spring, I can do something. If it's deafness, I can't. I don't fix ears.

Before you do anything radical to the dangblasted thing, test it one more time to make sure it really is not working. Put in a piece of white bread and set the dial on "dark." Now give it lots and lots of time to pop up. If it doesn't, take a table fork, jab it down in the toaster, spear the toast and pull it out manually. If you can't get the fork in fast enough and the toast catches on fire, pour the glass of water you have ready into the toaster and *put out the fire.* You now know without question that the toaster will not pop up on its own. But it still toasts even if it doesn't pop, and you can still use it.

Place the toaster on your breakfast table where you usually have it. Directly above toaster screw an eyehook into the ceiling. Put a drop of Krazy Glue on hook before placing it in ceiling. It will now hold toast up to 5,000 lbs. — or one bagel. Now take a piece of string and feed one end through the eyehook and let it dangle next to toaster. Attach the fishhook to that end of the string and tie the other end to a window-shade handle. You are now ready to use your toaster.

Fasten the fishhook into the crust and drop bread into toaster. When the toast starts to smoke, just pull on the string and the bread will come out toasted to perfection. You do not have to fool with any controls on the toaster anymore.

Warning Make sure no fish is still attached to fishhook. Use jam and margarine in your usual manner. Stay away from butter — too much cholesterol.

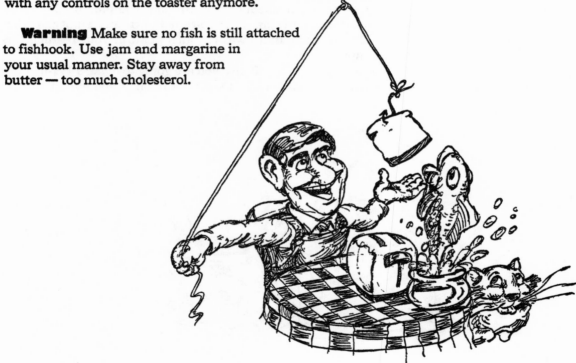

117

Installing a Vacuum Dirt Disposal

Tools and Supplies Upright vacuum cleaner, 20 ft. of vacuum attachment hose, electric wall drill.

This vacuum dirt disposal will eliminate forever the ugly job of emptying a vacuum cleaner bag. Instead, you plug the hose into each room as you clean. If you are not currently emptying vacuum cleaner bags, there wasn't much point in your reading this paragraph.

In each room of your house you are going to make a 1½-in. hole in the outside wall about 6 in. off the floor. If you live in a brick

house, then you will have to rent a masonry drill, but in any other kind of house a standard home drill will get you through the wall—if you stay with it. After each hole is made, be sure that the vacuum hose will fit into it. If not, then make the hole larger or smaller, as required. Next time I hope you'll measure first.

Now remove the bag from your vacuum cleaner and destroy it. You will never need it again. When you bought your vacuum, you should have received a part that fits where the bag went, so you could use the machine as a blowing unit to get dirt out of corners. If you threw it away with the box, your dealer can supply one. Next

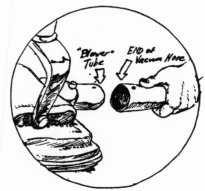

time, I hope you'll be more careful. If you can't get one from your dealer, you made a big mistake when you destroyed that vacuum cleaner bag. If you have a Hoover, ask a Hoover dealer. If you have a Eureka, ask a Eureka dealer. If you have a Royal, ask a Royal dealer, etc. If you have an Electrolux, don't ask anybody; these instructions won't work with that cleaner.

After you have the exhaust part connected where the bag once fit, slip one end of a 20-ft. hose into the end of the tube protruding from that part. The other end of the hose goes into the hole in the wall of the room you are cleaning. Now turn on the cleaner and start to vacuum the normal way. Look at all that filth from your floor going out through the hole in the wall to where it came from in the first place.

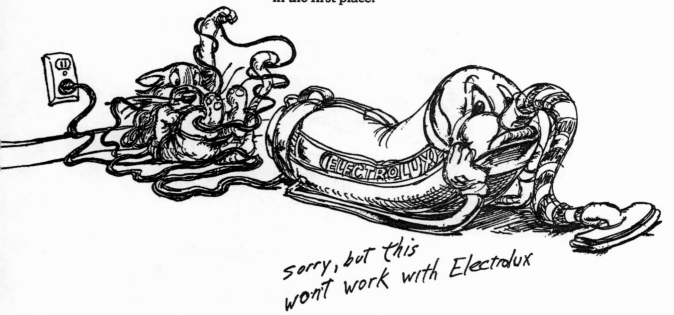

sorry, but this won't work with Electrolux

Caution Of course, the dirt will eventually come back in, but next time I hope you won't let it pile up the way you did in the past.

Don't Vacuum when anyone is walking by one of the holes.

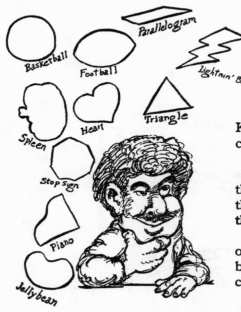

Basketball
Football
Parallelogram
Lightnin' Bolt
Spleen
Heart
Triangle
Stop Sign
Piano
Jellybean

Home Swimming Pool Installation

Tools and Supplies Two or three heavy plastic pool covers, Krazy Glue, tractor, Mr. Coffee filters, string, bricks (or deck chairs), 10,000 clay flowerpots and flowers.

I didn't have a swimming pool for a long time for two reasons: (1) the owner of the apartment where I lived would not let me tear up the laundry room floor, and (2) I forget — but I know it had something to do with my bridgework.

Finally I moved into my own house, and if you, too, are a home owner, you can follow my instructions and save yourself a real bundle of money from what so-called professional pool makers charge.

Outline Pool shape with string

First, decide on the shape of your pool. You might want to follow my creative lead. I built mine in the shape of a donut, completely round with a hole in the middle. This way you can't see either end from anywhere in the pool, so you think you are swimming much farther than you really are. Liberace has one in the shape of a piano, but I understand it is hard to make the strings sound under water. If you wish, you can try the conventional-shape pool to start. With my pool-building technique you can always change the shape when you get tired of it, which is something the so-called professional can't claim.

Outline the shape on the ground with some string so you will remember where you want to dig. Now rent a dirt-digging shovel tractor; I suggest a Caterpillar, model 972-11008-4DC. This one gets over 25 mi. to the gallon and has automatic transmission. I hate a stick shift.

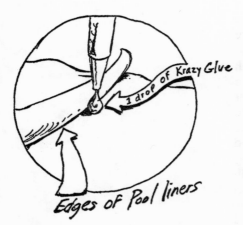

Edges of Pool liners

Always start the digging tractor from center out, *piling dirt on outside of the string marker,* well back from the hole. Unless you take too many coffee breaks, you can dig a good-sized hole in one hour. If you want it deeper in places, just dig deeper in the places you want it deeper. You can judge how deep you want it by the size of the people who are going to swim there. Anything deeper than 8 ft. is for very tall people.

Lay out your plastic pool liners on the ground and, with your Krazy Glue, cement two edges together, making a seam. This will hold a person weighing up to 5,000 lbs. Place the plastic liner in hole and smooth it over the bottom and sides so it takes the shape of the hole. Have a 4-in. flap hang over the top of the hole all the way around. Every few feet on this flap put a brick or a sun chair to hold it tight to the ground.

Now, with the garden hose, fill your pool with water. It will take a day and a night to fill it all the way, and the next day you will have a wonderful pool for swimming.

Start digging from center

I know what you are thinking. "Boy is that author a dummy. He builds this great pool and forgets to put in a filter." Well, I didn't forget, smarty. Just read on.

To clean pool water just take a Mr. Coffee filter in each hand and swim or walk around. You will collect all kinds of dirt in the filter. I find only genuine Mr. Coffee filters will do. The others make the pool taste funny.

Fill the 10,000 clay flowerpots you bought with the dirt you dug up to make the pool, plant flowers in them, and place them artistically around your pool and yard.

Warning Keep your fingernails and toenails cut as short as you can. If they catch in the plastic and make a hole, the water will slowly flow out of the pool and make your backyard into a swamp — with flowers.